Scholastic Success With
Spelling

Grade 1

by Lisa Molengraft

New York • Toronto • London • Auckland • Sydney
Mexico City • New Delhi • Hong Kong • Buenos Aires

Teaching *Resources*

Cover art by Amy Vangsgard
Cover design by Maria Lilja
Interior illustrations by Mark Mason
Interior design by Quack & Company

ISBN 0-439-55372-5

12 40 09

Scholastic Teaching Resources

About the Book

Parents and teachers alike will find this book to be a valuable learning tool. The book is organized into 21 lists, each following a phonetic spelling rule. The list words were developed from a collection of age-appropriate, high-priority word lists. At the end of each list you will find two words that can be used as an academic challenge.

Throughout the book you will find the following symbols that represent various strategy-based skills:

 Visual Discrimination Skills: *Use this strategy to highlight visual similarities among words.*

 Sound Relationship Skills: *Use this strategy to highlight sound patterns among words.*

 Dictation Skills: *Read the dictation sentence aloud to children. Having children write the sentence will give them additional practice in spelling list words as well as practice in using correct punctuation.*

 Writing Skills: *Use this strategy to practice writing sentences using the list words.*

 Reading Skills: *These activities include stories and letters with missing words, giving children an opportunity to connect reading with writing.*

 Fun Stuff!: *This section includes games, puzzles, and codes in which children apply previously learned strategies.*

 Challenge Word Activity: *This section offers an opportunity to stretch spelling skills to a more difficult level using the two optional challenge words.*

 Bright Idea Activities: *This section offers extension ideas to bridge learning beyond "the book" and into "the world."*

Throughout the book children will find Review Lists. These are not a collection of "old words," but are new list words that follow previously learned patterns. This list gives children a chance to apply mastered skills and strategies as they spell new words.

Through a collection of well-prepared lists, age-appropriate challenges, valuable spelling strategies, and stimulating activities, children will gain the self-confidence they need to become strong spellers.

Table of Contents

Apples! Apples!

 The **short-*a* sound** *is the beginning sound of the word* **apple**.

Read each list word. Circle the letter that makes the short-*a* sound.

 **Read.**

1. an
2. at
3. as
4. and
5. can
6. had

 Challenge Words

7. fast
8. lamp

 Copy.

1. _____
2. _____
3. _____
4. _____
5. _____
6. _____

7. _____
8. _____

 **Organize.**

list words that begin with *a*

_____

_____

_____

_____

list words with *a* in the middle

_____

_____

 Draw an (apple) around the list word that is spelled correctly.

1. an   un
2. cin   can
3. et   at
4. had   dah
5. as   az
6. nad   and

 Mom <u>and</u> Dad <u>had</u> <u>an</u> apple.

Scholastic Teaching Resources

 Use a list word to complete each sentence.

| at | had | an | can | as | and |

1. We went to _____ apple farm.

2. We picked green _____ red apples.

3. One apple was as big _____ a ball.

4. We _____ lots of fun!

5. We went home _____ dinnertime.

6. Now Mom _____ make apple pie.

Each list word is hidden two times. Circle the words.

hidanaastcan

kuhadtatiand

ashadinande

dahcaniatean

Write the challenge word that matches each clue.

I can be turned off and on. I am a _____.

I am not slow. I am _____.

 **Add a letter to the beginning of** as, an, **and** at **to make new words.**
Example an **words are** can, Dan, **and** fan.

Elephant Tricks

 *The **short**-*e* **sound** is the beginning sound of the word **elephant**.*

Read each list word. Circle the letter that makes the short *e* sound.

 **Read.**

1. end
2. get
3. let
4. red
5. ten
6. yes

🏆 **Challenge Words**

7. nest
8. went

 Copy.

1. _____
2. _____
3. _____
4. _____
5. _____
6. _____

7. _____
8. _____

 **Organize.**

list words with *en*

_____

_____

list words with *et*

_____

_____

other list words

_____

_____

 Write the list word that begins with the same sound as each picture.

1. _____

2. _____

3. _____

4. _____

5. _____

6. _____

 <u>Let</u> the <u>ten</u> <u>red</u> cats in at the <u>end</u>.

Scholastic Teaching Resources

Write the list word that matches each clue.

red
get
yes
let
end
ten

1. I am the opposite of *no*. I am _____.

2. I am a number. I am _____.

3. I am not the start. I am the _____.

4. I am a color. I am _____.

5. We rhyme with *jet*. We are _____ and _____.

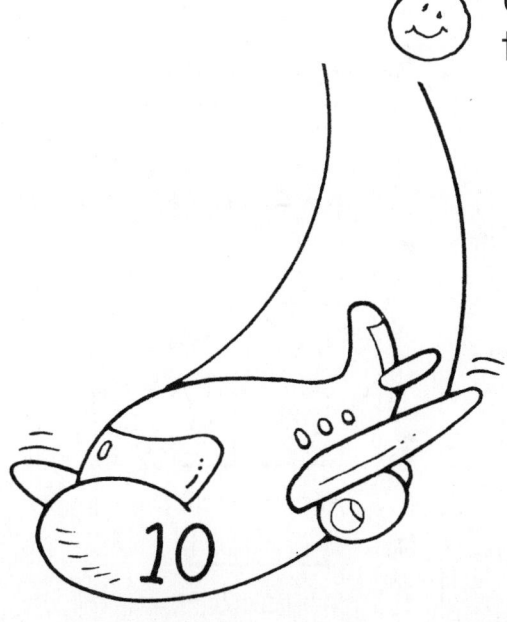

Unscramble the letters to spell the list words.

ent _____

der _____

teg _____

dne _____

sye _____

elt _____

 Write the challenge words in all uppercase letters. Then write them in all lowercase letters. Circle the word that shows your best handwriting.

_____   _____

_____   _____

On another sheet of paper, write a sentence using each of the list words.

Iggy the Inchworm

 The **short-*i* sound** is the beginning sound for the word **inchworm**

Read each list word. Circle the letter that makes the short-*i* sound.

 **Read.**   **Copy.**    **Organize.**

Read	Copy	Organize
1. if	**1.** _____	list words that begin with *i*
2. is	**2.** _____	_____
3. big	**3.** _____	_____
4. him	**4.** _____	list words that begin with *h*
5. his	**5.** _____	_____
6. sit	**6.** _____	_____

 Challenge Words

other list words

7. will   **7.** _____   _____

8. flip   **8.** _____   _____

 Write the list word that ends with the same sound as each picture.

1. 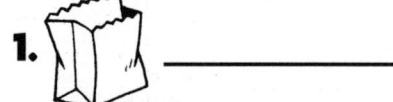 _____   **2.** 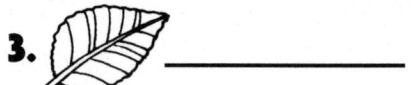 _____   **3.** _____

4.  _____   **5.**  _____ *and* _____

 <u>His</u> <u>big</u> pig <u>sits</u> in the mud.

Scholastic Teaching Resources

 Circle the six misspelled words. Write them correctly on the lines.

him	is	sit	his	if	big

Iggy the Inchworm

Tom has a new pet. It iz an inchworm. Hiz name is Iggy. Tom keeps hem in a cage. Iggy likes to sist on a leaf in the cage. Ef he eats the leaf, Iggy will grow beg.

1. _____   2. _____

3. _____   4. _____

5. _____   6. _____

 Write each list word in the shape box that fits it.

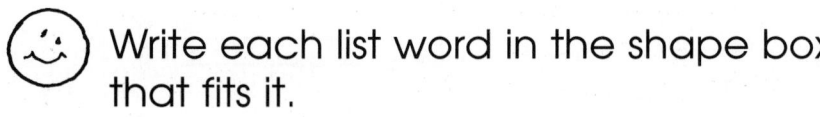

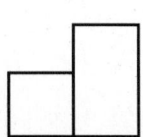 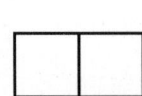 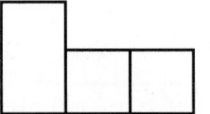

Each challenge word is hidden three times. Circle the words.

efliplithwill   **thewilltflip**

theriwillertt   **triflipwitrei**

 Cut letters from an old newspaper to spell each of the list words. Glue them on another sheet of paper and read them to a friend.

An Octopus

 *The **short-o** sound is the beginning sound of the word **octopus**.*

Read each list word. Circle the letter that makes the short-*o* sound.

 **Read.**

1. on

2. got

3. hop

4. fox

5. top

6. not

 Challenge Words

7. rock

8. stop

 Copy.

1. _____

2. _____

3. _____

4. _____

5. _____

6. _____

7. _____

8. _____

Organize.

list words with *op*

_____

_____

list words with *ot*

_____

_____

other list words

_____

_____

  Write the list word that matches each picture.

1.  _____

2.  _____

3. 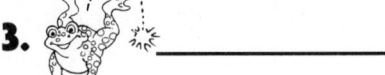 _____

4.  _____

 **The <u>fox</u> can <u>hop</u> to the <u>top</u>.**

 Use the list words to complete the letter.

fox	top	got	on	not	hop

Dear Todd,

I _____ to see an octopus on our trip.

It had two eyes on _____ of its head.

It was the color of a _____. We had to

_____ up _____ a rock to see it. Did

you know that an octopus is _____ a fish?

Your friend,

Bob

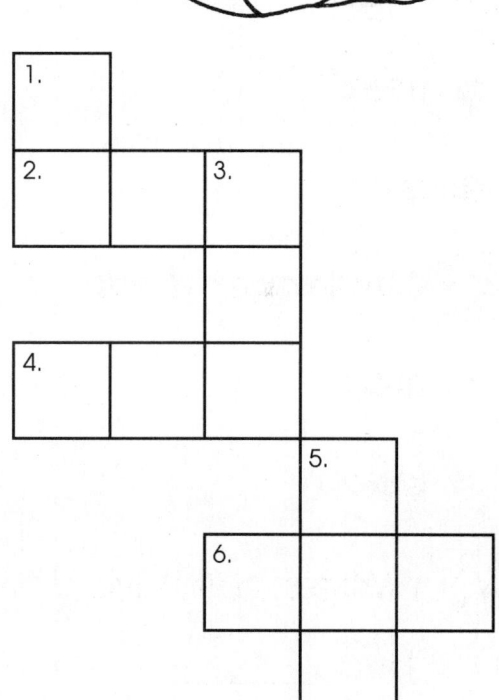

😊 Use the clues to complete the puzzle.

Across

2. I am _____ going.

4. 🐰

6. 🦊

Down

1. the opposite of *off*

3. the opposite of *bottom*

5. "I _____ it!"

⭐ On another sheet of paper, write each of the challenge words.
Draw a picture to illustrate each one.

 **On another sheet of paper, write the list words in alphabetical order.**

Umbrella Fun

➡ The **short-u sound** *is the beginning sound of the word* **umbrella**.

Read each list word. Circle the letter that makes the short-*u* sound.

 **Read.**

 Copy.

 **Organize.**

two-letter list word

1. up

1. _____

2. but

2. _____

_____

3. run

3. _____

three-letter list words

4. bug

4. _____

_____

5. mud

5. _____

_____

6. jump

6. _____

_____

 Challenge Words

_____

7. funny

7. _____

four-letter list word

8. puppy

8. _____

_____

 Write the list word that rhymes with each word.

1. bud _____

2. lump _____

3. hut _____

4. sun _____

5. tug _____

6. cup _____

 The <u>bug</u> can <u>run</u> and <u>jump</u> in the <u>mud</u>.

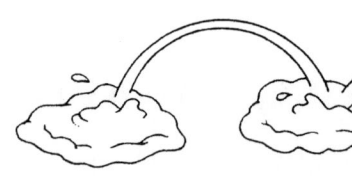

 Write two sentences using as many list words as you can.

_____

_____

 Unscramble the letters to spell the list words.

1. mupj _____

2. gbu _____

3. tub _____

4. nur _____

5. pu _____

6. dmu _____

Circle each list word hidden in the puzzle. The words go across, down, and diagonally.

up	bug
but	mud
run	jump

f	l	u	k	b	u	t	l
r	b	j	c	u	j	p	z
u	j	p	u	g	l	d	p
n	d	e	t	m	u	o	m
a	m	u	d	l	p	w	o

 Write each challenge word three times.

_____   _____   _____

_____   _____   _____

💡 **Look up each list word in a dictionary.**

Here Kitty!

 *Each of these pictures begins with a short vowel sound.*

a   e   i   o   u

Use the short vowel sounds to help you spell these new words.

 **Read.**   **Copy.**    **Organize.**

1. hat   1. _____   list words with short *a*

2. hand   2. _____   _____

3. men   3. _____   list word with short *e*

4. six   4. _____   _____

5. dog   5. _____   list word with short *i*

6. sun   6. _____   _____

 Challenge Words   list word with short *o*

7. happy   7. _____   _____

8. desk   8. _____   list word with short *u*

_____

 Write the list word that belongs in each group.

   4 5

1. _____   2. _____   3. _____

4. _____   5. _____   6. _____

 <u>Six</u> <u>men</u> with <u>hats</u> sat in the <u>sun</u>.

Scholastic Teaching Resources

✏ Write three sentences. Use two list words in each one.

_____

_____

_____

| sun |
| dog |
| six |
| men |
| hand |
| hat |

☺ **Where do cats go to learn?**

To find out, write the list word next to each picture. Then write the letters from the bold boxes in order on the line below to complete the answer.

Answer: Cats learn at kitty-_____!

 Write the challenge word that matches each clue.

I am not sad. I am _____.

I am a place to write. I am a _____.

 **On another sheet of paper, draw a picture. Hide pictures of the list words in the big picture. Make a list of the words and ask a friend to find all six hidden pictures.**

A Crazy Ape

 *The **long-*a* sound** is sometimes spelled* a_e *like in the word* **ape**.

Read each list word. Circle the long *a* and silent *e*.

 **Read.**   **Copy.**    **Organize.**

list words that rhyme

1. ate	**1.** _____	_____
2. make	**2.** _____	_____
3. came	**3.** _____	list words that do not rhyme
4. name	**4.** _____	
5. gave	**5.** _____	_____
6. tape	**6.** _____	_____

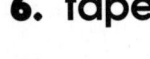 **Challenge Words**

7. frame	**7.** _____	_____
8. snake	**8.** _____	_____

 Circle each list word that is spelled correctly.

1. aet	ate	**2.** tape	taep	**3.** gave	gav
4. came	caym	**5.** mak	make	**6.** naem	name

 She <u>gave</u> us her <u>name</u> when she <u>came</u>.

Name _____

 Use a list word to complete the story.

ate	make	came	name	gave	tape

A Crazy Ape

We saw a new animal at the zoo. He is an ape. His _____

is Hairy. He _____ a banana. Next, he _____ over by me.

He _____ me his banana peel! Then he ripped my zoo map.

Follow the clues to play tic-tac-toe. As you find each answer, mark an *X* or *O*. The first to get three in a row is the winner!

1. I look like *cake*, but I begin with *m*. Mark an *X* on me.

2. I rhyme with *late*. Mark an *O* on me.

3. I begin like the word *got*. Mark an *X* on me.

4. I look like *ape*, but I begin with *t*. Mark an *O*.

5. I begin like the word *cake*. Mark an *X*.

6. I rhyme with the word *came*. Mark an *O*.

7. I am a challenge word. Mark an *X*.

came	ate	tape
snake	make	at
gave	as	name

 Write the challenge word that rhymes with each picture.

_____    _____

 **On another sheet of paper, scramble each of the list words and ask a friend to unscramble them.**

Let's Play in the Rain!

 The **long-**a **sound** *can be spelled with the letters* ay *like in the word* **may** *and the letters* ai *like in the word* **mail**.

Read each list word. Circle the letters that make the long-*a* sound.

Read.	**Copy.**	**Organize.**
1. day	1. _____	list words with long-*a* sound spelled *ay*
2. rain	2. _____	_____
3. tail	3. _____	_____
4. play	4. _____	_____
5. wait	5. _____	list words with long-*a* sound spelled *ai*
6. stay	6. _____	_____

 Challenge Words

7. away	7. _____	_____
8. chain	8. _____	_____

 Write the list word that begins with the same sound as the picture.

1. 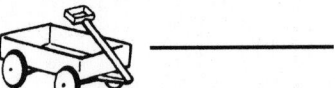 _____   2. 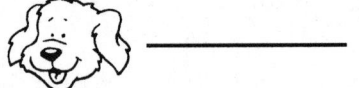 _____   3. 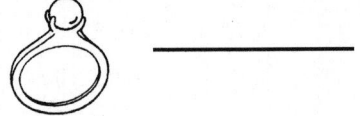 _____

4.  _____   5. 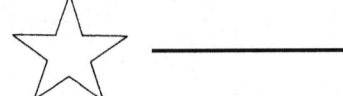 _____   6. 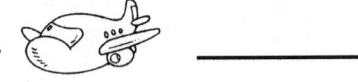 _____

 **We can <u>stay</u> to <u>play</u> in the <u>rain</u> one <u>day</u>.**

Scholastic Teaching Resources

 Write the list word that matches each clue.

| play | wait | day | rain | tail | stay |

1. I am wet and fall from the sky. I am _____.

2. I can be furry. I am a _____.

3. I have a morning and a night. I am a _____.

4. I am something you do with friends. I am _____.

5. We mean the same thing. We are _____ and _____.

Each list word is hidden two times. Circle the words.

aplayranwait   taywaitpday

watailinrain   plydayraintal

dystayentail   nplaysstayen

 Write the challenge words in all uppercase letters. Then write them in all lowercase letters. Circle the word that shows your best handwriting.

_____   _____

_____   _____

 **On another sheet of paper, write a story about a dog using as many list words as you can.**

Look Out! A Bee!

 *The* **long-***e* **sound** *can also be spelled with the letter* e *like in the word* **he** *and the letters* ee *like in the word* **need**.

Read each list word. Circle the letters that make the long-*e* sound.

Read.

1. me
2. tree
3. we
4. need
5. see
6. feet

🏆 **Challenge Words**

7. sleep
8. sheep

✏️ **Copy.**

1. _____
2. _____
3. _____
4. _____
5. _____
6. _____

7. _____
8. _____

🔤 **Organize.**

list words with long-*e* sound spelled *ee*

_____
_____
_____
_____
_____

list words with long-*e* sound spelled *e*

_____
_____

 Write the list word that begins with the same sound as each picture.

1. 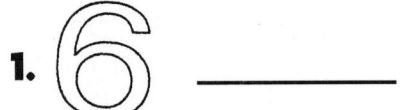 _____
2. 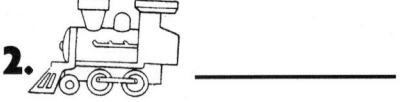 _____
3. 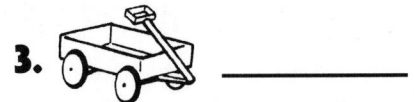 _____
4.  _____
5. 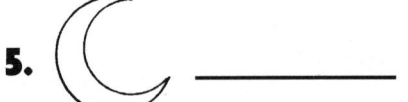 _____
6.  _____

 **We need to see the tree.**

Name _____

 Circle the six misspelled words. Write them correctly on the lines.

The Biggest Bee

One day my dad took mee on a hike.

"Do you seie that beehive in the big trea?" I asked.

"It is two feat long!" said my dad.

"We will ned a ladder to see," he said. We went up

the ladder, and a big bee came out. Whe ran!

| feet |
| me |
| we |
| tree |
| see |
| need |

1. _____   2. _____   3. _____

4. _____   5. _____   6. _____

 Use the clues to complete the puzzle.

Across
  2. We have two _____.
  5. Your eyes help you _____.
  6. I

Down
  1. We _____ food and shelter.
  3. a tall plant
  4. us

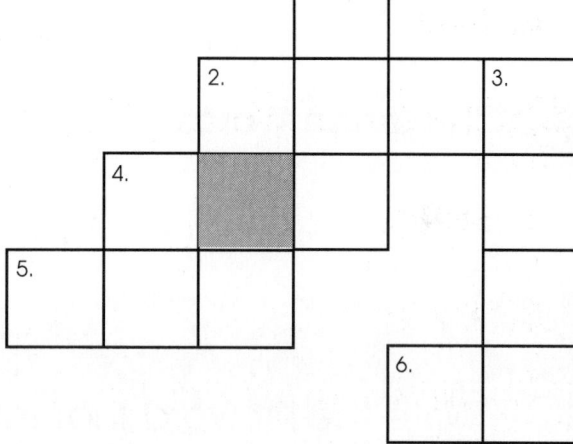

 Write the challenge word that matches each clue two times.

You do this at night.   _____ _____

You may count these at night.   _____ _____

 **Find each list word in some of your favorite books.**

Scholastic Teaching Resources

Ice Cream Truck

 The **long-*i* sound** *is can be spelled with the letters* i_e *like in the word* **ice** *and the letter* y *like in the word* **try**.

Read each list word. Circle the letter that makes the long-*i* sound.

 **Read.**   **Copy.**    **Organize.**

list words with *i_e*

Read	Copy
1. by	**1.** _____
2. like	**2.** _____
3. I	**3.** _____
4. my	**4.** _____
5. kite	**5.** _____
6. fly	**6.** _____

_____

_____

list words with *y*

_____

_____

_____

 Challenge Words

7. time	**7.** _____
8. hi	**8.** _____

the shortest list word

_____

 Write the list word that rhymes with each picture.

1. 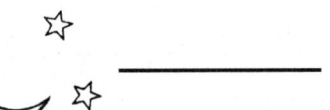 _____   **2.** 🌙 _____

 Write four list words that rhyme with each other.

_____   _____   _____   _____

 **I try to fly a kite by my house.**

Scholastic Teaching Resources

Name _____

 Use a list word to complete the poem.

Ice Cream Truck

Ding! Ding! Ding!

_____ hear the ice cream truck!

I can't believe _____ good luck.

When the truck comes _____,

Like a bird I _____.

I stop flying my _____,

So I can take a bite.

I _____ ice cream a lot!

| kite |
| my |
| I |
| by |
| like |
| fly |

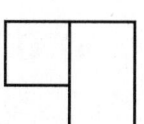 Write each list word in the shape box that fits it.

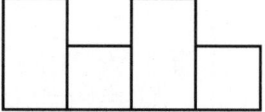 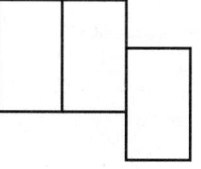

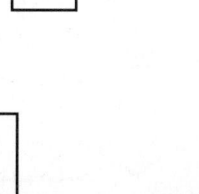

 Draw a picture showing each challenge word. Write each word.

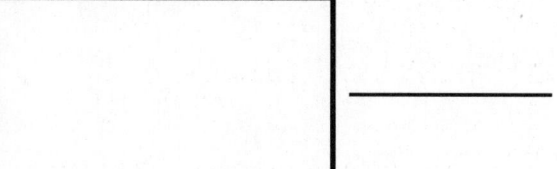 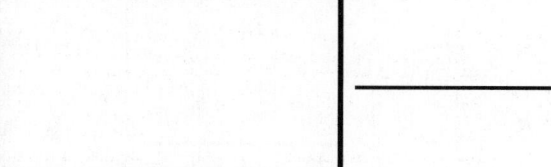

 **On another sheet of paper, make a word search using the list words.**

Oh, Ovals!

 The **long-**o **sound** is sometimes spelled with the letter o like in the word **no** and the letters o_e like in the word **cone**.

Read each list word. Circle the letters that make the long-o sound.

 **Read.**

1. so

2. home

3. go

4. bone

5. note

6. rope

 Challenge Words

7. vote

8. stone

 Copy.

1. _____

2. _____

3. _____

4. _____

5. _____

6. _____

7. _____

8. _____

 **Organize.**

list words with long-o sound spelled o_e

_____

_____

_____

_____

list words with long-o sound spelled o

_____

 Write the list word with the same ending sound as each picture.

1.  _____

2. 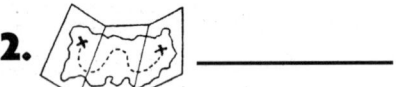 _____

3.  _____

4.  _____

5.  _____   *and* _____

 **I have a <u>note</u> to <u>go</u> <u>home</u>.**

Scholastic Teaching Resources

Write a sentence using as many list words as you can.

_____

☺ Unscramble the letters to spell the list words.

1. nebo _____

2. os _____

3. meho _____

4. pero _____

5. teon _____

6. og _____

☺ Circle each list word hidden in the puzzle. The words go across, down, and diagonally.

go	so
bone	rope
note	home

e	i	h	o	m	e	s	u
r	o	m	b	b	d	j	r
f	e	h	p	o	c	s	o
q	n	o	t	e	n	t	p
g	l	n	g	o	k	e	e

☆ Write each challenge word three times.

_____   _____   _____

_____   _____   _____

 Cut letters from a newspaper to spell each list word. Glue them on another sheet of paper and read them to someone at home.

A Tight Squeeze

 *The long vowel sounds can be spelled with the following letters:*

long *a*:	long *e*:	long *i*:	long *o*:
a_e, ay, ai	ee	i_e	o_e

Use the long vowel sound to help you spell these new words.

 **Read.**   ✏️ **Copy.**   🔤 **Organize.**

list words with
long-*a* sound

1. cake   **1.** _____   _____

2. nail   **2.** _____   _____

3. tray   **3.** _____   _____

4. seed   **4.** _____

list word with
long-*e* sound

5. nine   **5.** _____   _____

6. nose   **6.** _____

list word with
long-*i* sound

🏆 **Challenge Words**

_____

7. have   **7.** _____

list word with
long-*o* sound

8. here   **8.** _____

_____

 Write the list word that belongs in each group.

1.  _____   **2.** 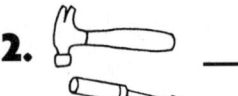 _____   **3.** 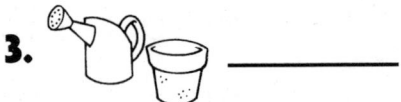 _____

4. _____   **5.** 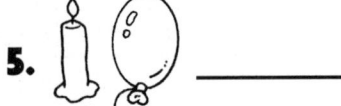 _____   **6.** 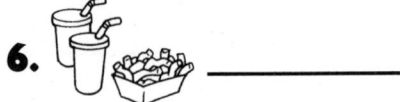 _____

 **The <u>cake</u> on the <u>tray</u> has <u>nine</u> candles.**

Scholastic Teaching Resources

Write three sentences. Use two list words in each one.

tray   seed   nose   cake   nine   nail

_____

_____

_____

What kind of cow can get through the farmer's fence?

To find out, write the list word next to each picture. Then write the letters from the bold boxes in order on the line below to answer the riddle.

Answer: A _____ cow!

Change one letter to turn each word into a challenge word.

hive _____   hire _____

On another sheet of paper, draw a picture. Hide pictures of the list words in the picture. Make a list of the words and ask a friend to find all six hidden pictures.

Scholastic Teaching Resources

Those Thorns!

 *The letters* th *make the sound at the beginning of the word* **thorn**.

Read each list word. Circle the letters *th* in each word.

 **Read.**

1. the

2. this

3. with

4. then

5. bath

6. that

 Challenge Words

7. them

8. they

 Copy.

1. _____

2. _____

3. _____

4. _____

5. _____

6. _____

7. _____

8. _____

 **Organize.**

list words that begin with *th*

_____

_____

_____

_____

list words that end with *th*

_____

_____

 Write the list word that rhymes with each word.

1. math _____   2. den _____   3. rat _____

 Unscramble each list word.

4. het _____   5. hiwt _____   6. tsih _____

 <u>That</u> baby took a <u>bath</u> <u>with</u> <u>this</u> toy.

 Circle the list word that completes each sentence. Then write it on the line.

"Mom, may I pick _____ flower?"   with   then   this

"Yes, but _____ flower has thorns."   then   that   bath

"But it is _____ prettiest one."   the   this   that

"_____ be careful."   With   Then   The

"Let's put it in a glass _____ water."   this   bath   with

"Yes, like it is taking a _____!"   with   the   bath

 Use the code to spell each list word.

n	i	h	w	t	b	e	s	a
1	2	3	4	5	6	7	8	9

1. ___ ___ ___ ___
   5   3   9   5

2. ___ ___ ___ ___
   6   9   5   3

3. ___ ___ ___ ___
   5   3   2   8

4. ___ ___ ___ ___
   5   3   7   1

5. ___ ___ ___
   5   3   7

6. ___ ___ ___ ___
   4   2   5   3

 Look closely at the spelling of the challenge words.

How are the two words alike? _____

How are they different? _____

💡 **Spell each list word aloud at the dinner table.**

Shiny Shells

The letters sh *make the sound at the beginning of the word* **shell**.

Read each list word. Circle the letters *sh* in each word.

 **Read.**   **Copy.**    **Organize.**

list words that
begin with *sh*

Read.	Copy.
1. ship	1. _____
2. she	2. _____
3. fish	3. _____
4. shape	4. _____
5. wish	5. _____
6. brush	6. _____

_____

_____

_____

list words that
end with *sh*

 **Challenge Words**

7. shine	7. _____
8. shoe	8. _____

_____

_____

_____

Draw a (shell) around the list word that is spelled correctly.

1. shipe   ship   **2.** shape   shap   **3.** she   shee

4. fish   fich   **5.** brosh   brush   **6.** wich   wish

 <u>She</u> saw the <u>shape</u> of a <u>fish</u> by the <u>ship</u>.

Scholastic Teaching Resources

 Write the list word that matches each clue.

fish   she   brush   ship   shape   wish

1. I live in water. I am a _____.

2. I am a name for a girl. I am _____.

3. I am used in hair. I am a _____.

4. I sail in the water. I am a _____.

5. I may be a circle or square. I am a _____.

6. Make me when you see a star. I am a _____.

Find each list word hidden two times. Circle the words.

shiwishashem   beshapeshwish

fibrushshipe   shfishishapen

weshelshipsho   brushshifish

 Write the challenge word that rhymes with each picture two times.

 _____   _____

_____   _____

 **On another sheet of paper, scramble the list words. Ask someone at home to unscramble them.**

Changing Gears

 *The letters* ch *make the sound at the beginning of the word* **chain**.
The letters wh *make the sound at the beginning of the word* **wheel**.

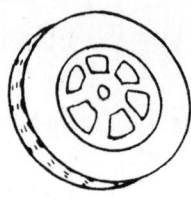

Read each list word. Circle the letters *ch* and *wh* in each word.

Read.   **Copy.**   **Organize.**

Read.	Copy.	Organize.
1. chin	**1.** _____	list words that begin with *ch*
2. chop	**2.** _____	_____
3. whale	**3.** _____	_____
4. when	**4.** _____	list words that begin with *wh*
5. inch	**5.** _____	_____
6. which	**6.** _____	_____

Challenge Words

list words that end with *ch*

7. why	**7.** _____	_____
8. what	**8.** _____	_____

Write the list word that rhymes with each word.

1. tail _____   **2.** mop _____   **3.** pinch _____

4. pitch _____   **5.** pen _____   **6.** win _____

 <u>Which</u> <u>whale</u> was an <u>inch</u> from the boat?

📖 Circle the five misspelled words. Write them correctly on the lines.

Dear Sam,

   I got a new bike for my birthday! It is painted like an orca wale. It is an ich longer than my old bike. Wen I got on it the first time, I nearly fell off! The next time I bumped my chen on the handlebars! Now I can ride great, wich took a lot of work. I even go through puddles super fast!

                        Your friend,

                        Stephen

1. _____

2. _____

3. _____

4. _____

5. _____

☺ Use the clues to complete the puzzle.

Across

   2. rhymes with *itch*

   4. found on a ruler

   5. _____ will we go?

Down

   1. part of a face

   2. ocean animal

   3. rhymes with *shop*

 Find each challenge word hidden three times. Circle the words.

whiwhatwhtat   whtwhywhyatt

whywhttwhatt   wywhtwhatwy

 **Which list words do you think are the hardest to spell?** On another sheet of paper, write the words in order from the easiest to the hardest to spell.

In My Backpack

 The letters ck *make the sound at the end of the word* **pick**.

Read each list word. Circle the letters *ck* in each word.

 **Read.**   **Copy.**    **Organize.**

Read.	Copy.	Organize.
1. duck	1. _____	list words with short-*a* sound
2. pack	2. _____	_____
3. stick	3. _____	_____
4. back	4. _____	list word with short-*e* sound
5. neck	5. _____	_____
6. rock	6. _____	list word with short-*i* sound

 Challenge Words

		list word with short-*o* sound
7. clock	7. _____	_____
8. quick	8. _____	list word with short-*u* sound
		_____

list word with short-*i* sound
_____

list word with short-*o* sound
_____

list word with short-*u* sound
_____

 Write the list word that matches each picture.

1.  _____   2.  _____   3.  _____

4. 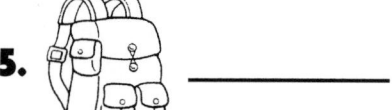 _____   5.  _____   6.  _____

 **The <u>duck</u> sat on the <u>rock</u> near the <u>stick</u>.**

 Use list words to complete the story.

In My Backpack

I went to the park with my friend Ben. We always

_____ some bread to feed the ducks. We sat on

a _____ near the water. Soon a white _____

swam up to us. It had a ring around its _____. It

came up to my backpack. It put its head in my

_____pack and found the bread! We let it _____

its head in again. It ate all of the bread! It was funny!

neck
pack
rock
duck
stick
back

 Write each list word in the shape box that fits it. Then use the number code to spell out what is in the backpack.

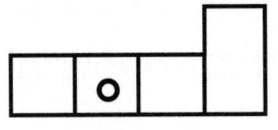
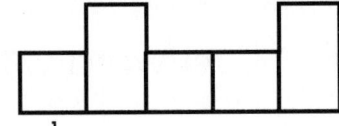
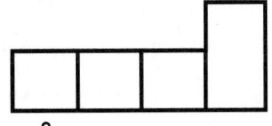

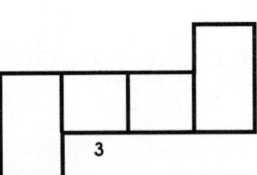
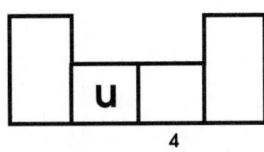
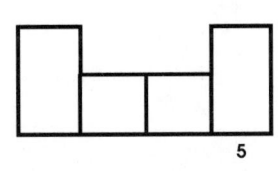

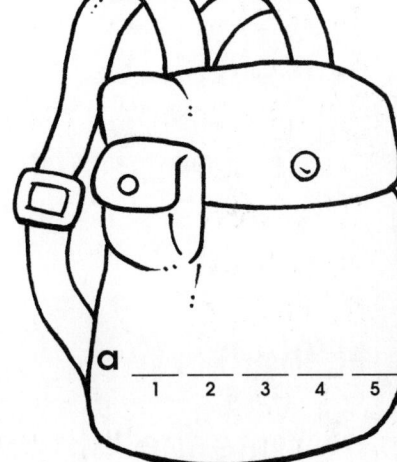

Write the challenge word that matches each clue.

an instrument that tells time _____

fast _____

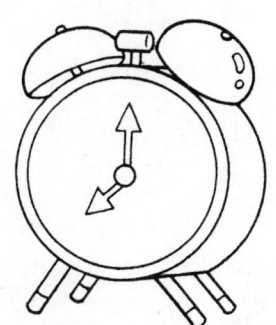

 **On another sheet of paper, write the list words in alphabetical order.**

Shopping Spree

These two letters work together to make one sound.

  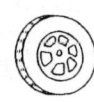 

th   sh   ch   wh   ck

Use the letter sounds to help you spell these new words.

 **Read.**   **Copy.**    **Organize.**

list words with short-*a* sound

Read	Copy
1. shop	1. _____
2. chip	2. _____
3. dish	3. _____
4. white	4. _____
5. black	5. _____
6. math	6. _____

_____

_____

list words with short-*i* sound

_____

_____

_____

 Challenge Words

other list words

7. chick   7. _____

_____

8. thank   8. _____

_____

_____

 Write the list word that fits in each group.

1.  _____   2. _____   3. _____

4. _____   5. _____   6. _____

 **I got the black and white dish at the shop.**

Scholastic Teaching Resources

Write three sentences. Use two list words in each one.

| black | dish | shop | white | math | chip |

_____

_____

_____

How do you make a shop hop?

To find out, write the list word that rhymes with each picture. Then write the words from the bold boxes in order on the lines below.

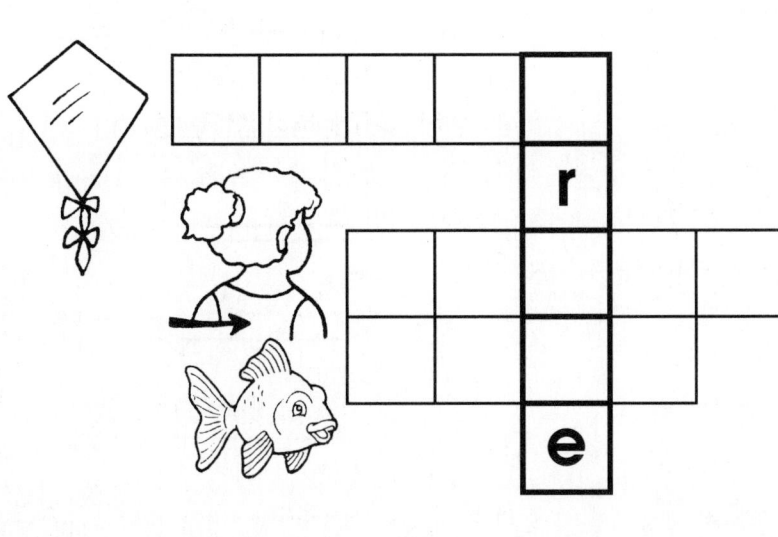

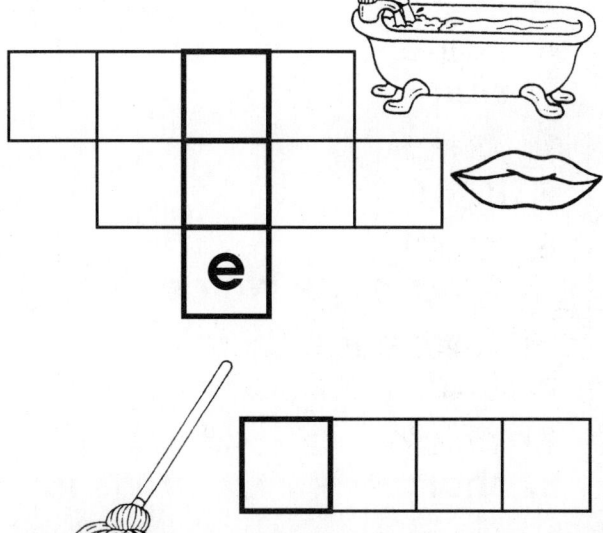

Answer: __ __ __ __ __   __ __ __ __ __ !

 Change two letters to turn each word into a challenge word.

thing _____   **crack** _____

 **On another sheet of paper, write a definition for each list word.**

Scholastic Teaching Resources

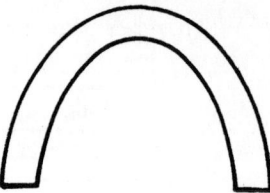

Under the Arch

 *The letters* ar *make the sound at the beginning of the word* **arch**.

Read each list word. Circle the letters *ar* in each word.

 Read.

1. are
2. hard
3. star
4. jar
5. part
6. farm

 Challenge Words

7. start
8. shark

 **Copy.**

1. _____
2. _____
3. _____
4. _____
5. _____
6. _____

7. _____
8. _____

Organize.

list words with
ar in the middle

_____

_____

_____

other list words

_____

_____

_____

 Write the list word that rhymes with each word.

1. card _____   2. art _____   3. harm _____

4. car _____ *and* _____ *and* _____

 **That <u>part</u> of the <u>star</u> is <u>hard</u> to see.**

Hide two list words in these boxes.

1.

2.

 Find each list word hidden two times. Circle the words.

hapartjardar   pahardoraret

fastararfarm   arfarmareth

stjartstarernt   tehardetpart

 Unscramble the letters to spell the list words.

raj _____   amrf _____   dhra _____

trap _____   rea _____   rast _____

Draw a picture showing each challenge word. Write each challenge word as a title for its matching picture.

_____   _____

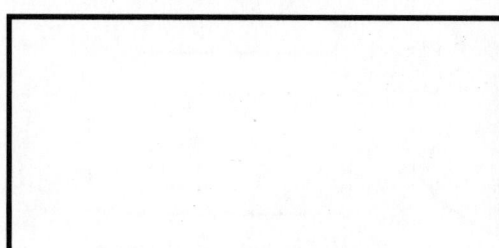

 **On another sheet of paper, change one letter in each list word to make a new word. For example:** jar **becomes** jam **or** far.

Ornaments Galore

 *The letters* or *make the sound at the beginning of the word* **ornament.**

Read each list word. Circle the letters *or* in each word.

 Read.

1. or

2. corn

3. porch

4. horn

5. for

6. short

 Challenge Words

7. your

8. horse

 **Copy.**

1. _____

2. _____

3. _____

4. _____

5. _____

6. _____

7. _____

8. _____

Organize.

two- or three-letter
list words

_____

_____

four- or five-letter
list words

_____

_____

_____

_____

_____

 Write the list word that begins with the same sound as each picture.

1. 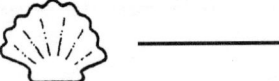 _____

2. 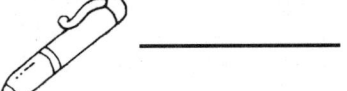 _____

3. 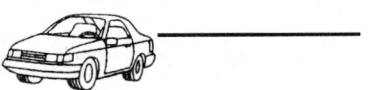 _____

4. 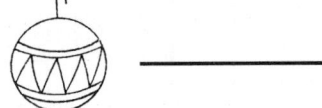 _____

5.  _____

6. _____

 **We eat <u>corn</u> <u>or</u> cake on the <u>porch</u> <u>for</u> lunch.**

Scholastic Teaching Resources

 Use the list words to complete the story.

for	or	porch	short	horn	corn

Let's Do It Again!

I had a great holiday. We ate turkey and _____ for dinner.

Then we played a _____ game. Later, we heard the

_____ of a car outside. It was Uncle Norm. He stepped on the

_____, and we all hugged him. He had a big box. Could it be

for my brother _____ me? It was full of ornaments _____

the tree. We all helped hang them before we went to bed. I hope

we can do it all again tomorrow!

Circle each list word hidden in the puzzle. The words go across
and down. How many times can you find the word *or* in the
puzzle? _____

s	b	k	c	l	h	m	b
h	e	p	o	r	c	h	t
o	t	s	r	f	a	o	s
r	g	i	n	k	j	r	l
t	l	f	o	r	e	n	u

 Look closely at the spelling of the challenge words.

How are the two words alike? _____

How are they different? _____

 **Find each list word in some of your favorite books.**

To You, From Me

 *The letter* o *can be used to make other sounds such as* oo *like in the words* **to** *and* **do** *and* ∪ *like in the words* **of**, **from**, *and* **love**.

Read each list word. Circle the letter *o* in each word.

 **Read.**

1. to

2. do

3. you

4. of

5. from

6. love

🏆 **Challenge Words**

7. come

8. some

✏️ **Copy.**

1. _____

2. _____

3. _____

4. _____

5. _____

6. _____

7. _____

8. _____

🧱 **Organize.**

list words with
short-*u* sound

_____

_____

_____

list words with
oo (moo) sound

_____

_____

_____

 Draw a heart around the list word that is spelled correctly.

1. luv   love

2. you   yoo

3. uv   of

4. to   tu

5. frum   from

6. du   do

 <u>Do</u> <u>you</u> <u>love</u> <u>to</u> get cards <u>from</u> your friends?

Scholastic Teaching Resources

Use the list words to complete the valentine cards. Be careful! These words are not spelled the way they sound.

_____ my teacher,

Thank _____

for being so nice!

Nicki

Dear Jack,

_____ you

want to be my

friend?

_____,

Sam

To Anna,

You are one

_____ my

best friends.

_____,

Rosa

Follow the clues to play tic-tac-toe. As you find each answer, mark an *X* or *O*. The first to get three in a row is the winner!

1. I look like the word *dove* except I begin with *l*. Mark an *X* on me.

2. I rhyme with the word *love*. Mark an *O*.

3. I begin like the word *time*. Mark an *X*.

4. I have three letters. Mark an *O*.

5. I begin like the word *dog*. Mark an *X*.

6. I am the opposite of *to*. Mark an *O*.

7. I am a challenge word that begins with the letter *c*. Mark an *X*.

8. I am a challenge word that begins with the letter *s*. Mark an *O*.

you	love	come
some	from	I
of	to	do

Write the challenge words in all uppercase letters. Then write them in all lowercase letters. Circle the word that shows your best handwriting.

_____ _____ _____

On another sheet of paper, write the list words in alphabetical order.

Under Control

 *The letters* ar *make the sound at the beginning of the word* **arch**.
The letters or *make the sound at the beginning of the word* **ornament**.

Use the letter sounds to help you spell these new words.

 **Read.**   **Copy.**    **Organize.**

list words with
ar sound

1. car   **1.** _____   _____

2. fork   **2.** _____   _____

3. arm   **3.** _____   _____

4. thorn   **4.** _____   _____

5. north   **5.** _____

list words with
or sound

6. park   **6.** _____   _____

 Challenge Words

                                          _____

7. store   **7.** _____   _____

8. world   **8.** _____   _____

 Write the list word that ends with the same sound as each picture.

1. 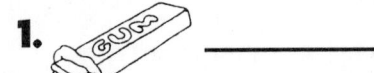 _____   **2.**  _____   **3.** 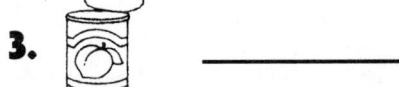 _____

4.  _____   **5.**  _____ *and* _____

 Park the car north of the fork in the road.

Scholastic Teaching Resources

Write three sentences using as many list words as you can.

_____

_____

_____

Use the code to spell each of the list words.

t	n	c	h	a	f	r	p	k	m	o
1	2	3	4	5	6	7	8	9	10	11

 2   11   7   1   4   5   7   10

 1   4   11   7   2

 3   5   7

 8   5   7   9

 6   11   7   9

 Change two letters in each word to make a challenge word.

slope _____   **worth** _____

 **Look up the list words in a dictionary. On another sheet of paper, write each word and the page number where each is found.**

Name _____

Master Spelling List

an	do	if	or	tape
and	dog	inch	pack	ten
are	duck	is	park	that
arm	end	jar	part	the
as	farm	jump	play	then
at	feet	kite	porch	this
ate	fish	let	rain	thorn
back	fly	like	red	to
bath	for	love	rock	top
big	fork	make	rope	tray
black	fox	math	run	tree
bone	from	me	see	up
brush	gave	men	seed	wait
bug	get	mud	shape	we
but	go	my	she	whale
by	got	nail	ship	when
cake	had	name	shop	which
came	hand	neck	short	white
can	hard	need	sit	wish
car	hat	nine	six	with
chin	him	north	so	yes
chip	his	nose	star	you
chop	home	not	stay	
corn	hop	note	stick	
day	horn	of	sun	
dish	I	on	tail	

Scholastic Teaching Resources

Page 4
begin with a: an, at, as, and; a in the middle: can, had; 1. an; 2. can; 3. at; 4. had; 5. as; 6. and

Page 5
1. an; 2. and; 3. as; 4. had; 5. at; 6. can;
hid**an**a**as**t**can**;
ku**had**tati**and**;
ash**ad**in**and**e;
dah**can**i**at**e**an**; lamp, fast

Page 6
en: end, ten; et: get, let; other: red, yes; 1. red; 2. yes; 3. get; 4. let; 5. ten; 6. end

Page 7
1. yes; 2. ten; 3. end; 4. red; 5. get, let; ten, red, get, end, yes, let

Page 8
i: if, is; h: him, his; other: big, sit; 1. big; 2. him; 3. if; 4. sit; 5. is, his

Page 9
1. is; 2. His; 3. him; 4. sit; 5. If; 6. big;
big, sit, him, if, is, his;
e**flip**lith**will**;
the**will**t**flip**; theri**will**ertt;
tri**flip**witrei

Page 10
op: hop, top; ot: got, not; other: on, fox; 1. top; 2. fox; 3. hop; 4. on

Page 11
got, top, fox, hop, on, not

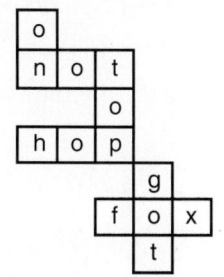

Page 12
two-letter: up; three-letter: but, run, bug, mud; four-letter: jump; 1. mud; 2. jump; 3. but; 4. run; 5. bug; 6. up

Page 13
Sentences will vary.
1. jump, 2. bug, 3. but, 4. run; 5. up, 6. mud

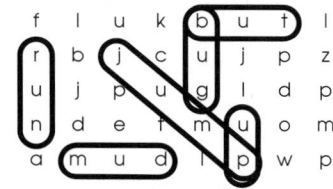

Page 14
a: hat, hand; e: men; i: six; o: dog; u: sun; 1. sun; 2. six; 3. hat; 4. hand; 5. men; 6. dog

Page 15
Sentences will vary.

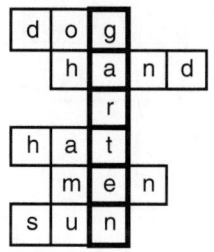

kitty-garten!;
happy, desk

Page 16
rhyme: came, name; do not rhyme: ate, make, gave, tape; 1. ate; 2. tape; 3. gave; 4. came; 5. make; 6. name

Page 17
name, ate, came, gave

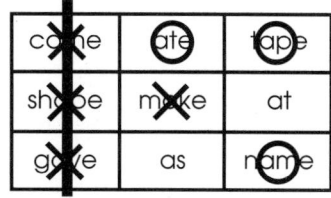

snake, frame

Page 18
ay: day, play, stay; ai: rain, tail, wait; 1. wait; 2. day; 3. rain; 4. tail; 5. stay; 6. play

Page 19
1. rain; 2. tail; 3. day; 4. play; 5. wait, stay;
a**play**ran**wait**,
tay**wait**p**day**;
wat**ail**in**rain**,
ply**dayrain**tal;
dy**stay**ent**ail**,
n**play**s**stay**en

Page 20
ee: tree, need, see, feet; e: me, we; 1. see; 2. tree; 3. we; 4. feet; 5. me; 6. need

Page 21
1. me; 2. see; 3. tree; 4. feet; 5. need; 6. We

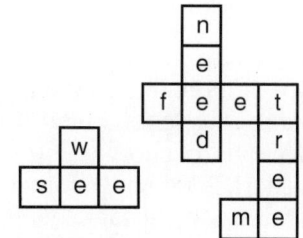

sleep; sheep

Page 22
i_e: like, kite; y: by, my, fly; shortest: I; 1. like; 2. kite; by, I, my, fly

Page 23
I, my, by, fly, kite, like; my, like, fly; I, kite, by

Page 24
o_e: home, bone, note, rope; o: so, go; 1. note; 2. rope; 3. home; 4. bone; 5. so, go

Page 25
Sentences will vary.
1. bone; 2. so; 3. home; 4. rope; 5. note; 6. go

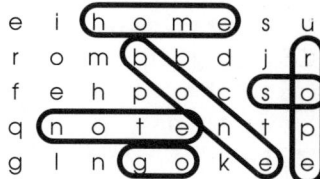

Page 26
a: cake, nail, tray; e: seed; i: nine; o: nose; 1. nose; 2. nail; 3. seed; 4. nine; 5. cake; 6. tray

Page 27
Sentences will vary.

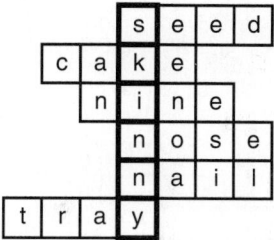

skinny;
have, here

Page 28
begin with th: the, this, then, that; end with th: with, bath; 1. bath; 2. then; 3. that; 4. the; 5. with; 6. this

Page 29
this, that, the, Then, with, bath; 1. that; 2. bath; 3. this; 4. then; 5.the; 6. with;
They both begin with the letters **the**. One ends with m, and one ends with y.

Page 30

begin with sh: ship, she, shape; end with sh: fish, wish, brush; 1. ship; 2. shape; 3. she; 4. fish; 5. brush; 6. wish

Page 31

1. fish; 2. she; 3. brush; 4. ship; 5. shape; 6. wish; shi**wish**ashe**m**, be**shape**sh**wish**; fi**brush**sh**ip**e, shf**ish**i**shape**n; we**shelship**sho, **brush**shif**ish**; shoe, shine

Page 32

begin with ch: chin, chop; begin with wh: whale, when, which; end with ch: inch, which; 1. whale; 2. chop; 3. inch; 4. which; 5. when; 6. chin

Page 33

1. whale; 2. inch; 3. When; 4. chin; 5. which

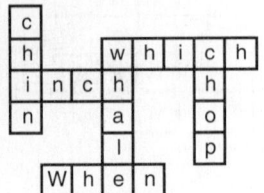

whi**what**whtat, wht**whywhy**att; **why**whtt**what**t, wywht**what**wy

Page 34

short a: pack, back; short e: neck; short i: stick; short o: rock; short u: duck; 1. neck; 2. duck; 3. stick; 4. rock; 5. pack; 6. back

Page 35

pack, rock, duck, neck, back, stick; rock, stick, neck; pack, duck, back; snack; clock, quick

Page 36

short **a**: black, math; short **i**: chip, dish; other: white, shop; 1. shop; 2. dish; 3. math; 4. chip; 5. white; 6. black

Page 37

Sentences will vary.

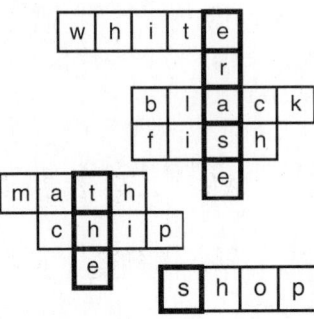

erase the s; thank, chick

Page 38

ar in the middle: hard, part, farm; other: are, star, jar; 1. hard; 2. part; 3. farm; 4. are, star, jar

Page 39

1.-2. Answers will vary. ha**partjar**dar, pa**hard**ora**re**t, fa**star**ar**farm**, ar**farmare**th, st**jartstar**ernt, te**hard**et**part**; jar, farm, hard; part, are, star

Page 40

two- or three-letter: or, for; four- or five-letter: corn, porch, horn, short; 1. short; 2. porch; 3. corn; 4. horn; 5. or; 6. for

Page 41

corn, short, horn, porch, or, for

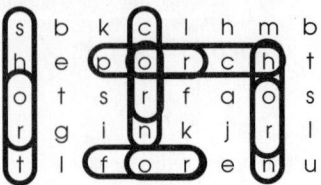

5 times; They both have the **or** sound. **Your** is spelled **our** and **horse** is spelled **or**.

Page 42

short u: of, from, love; oo: to, do, you; 1. love; 2. you; 3. of; 4. to; 5. from; 6. do

Page 43

To you; Do, From; of, Love

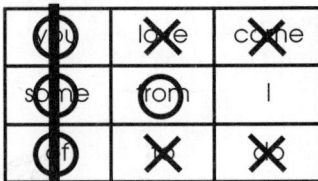

Page 44

ar: car, arm, park; or: fork, thorn, north; 1. arm; 2. north; 3. thorn; 4. car; 5. fork, park

Page 45

Sentences will vary. north, arm, thorn, car, park, fork; store, world